DISCOVERING
TREES

D0473858

DOUGLAS FLORIAN

ALADDIN BOOKS

Macmillan Publishing Company   New York
Collier Macmillan Publishers   London

Trees are the largest living things in the world. They are even bigger than whales.

The heaviest tree of all is the giant sequoia (see-kwoy-ah). One sequoia is called "General Sherman." It weighs two million pounds and is 270 feet high.

The tallest tree in the world is the California redwood. It can grow to be 400 feet high.

Some trees are very old. One cypress tree in Mexico is thought to be about 5,000 years old. Its trunk is 90 feet around.

Giant Sequoias

A tree begins its life as a seed. A small root grows from the seed down into the soil. Then a stem and leaves grow above the soil. This baby tree is called a *seedling*. As the tree grows, the stem gets thicker and harder. After some time the stem has become hard enough to be called wood. This wooden stem is called a *trunk*. The trunk of the red gum tree in Australia can reach 200 feet.

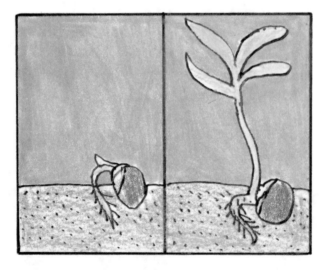

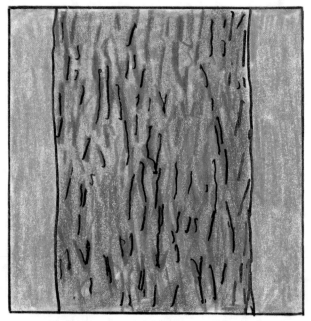

BLACK WALNUT

The trunk of a tree is covered by a hard layer of dead wood called the *outer bark*. Bark protects a tree from insects and animals. It keeps the inside of the tree from getting too dry or too cold. It can even protect a tree from a forest fire.

The outer bark of a tree is not alive. When the tree trunk grows wider, the bark, which does not grow, must either crack or peel off.

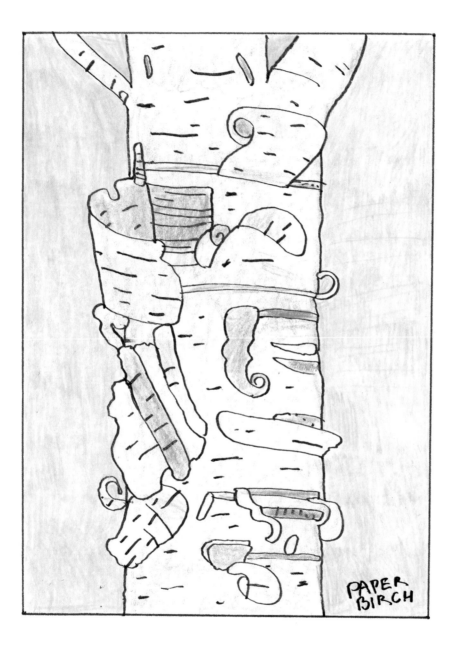

This river birch tree's bark is peeling off like sheets of paper.

Under the outer bark is a living *inner bark*. And under that is a layer of wood called *sapwood*. The sapwood carries a mixture of water and minerals called sap from the roots to the leaves. Under the sapwood is a darker wood called *heartwood*. This hard wood helps keep the tree standing.

Each year the tree's trunk grows thicker. If you look at a tree stump, you can see its *tree rings*. Each pair of rings tells you how much the tree grew in one year. If you add up the pairs, you'll know how old the tree is. The light-colored rings show the tree's growth each spring. The dark rings show the growth in summer.

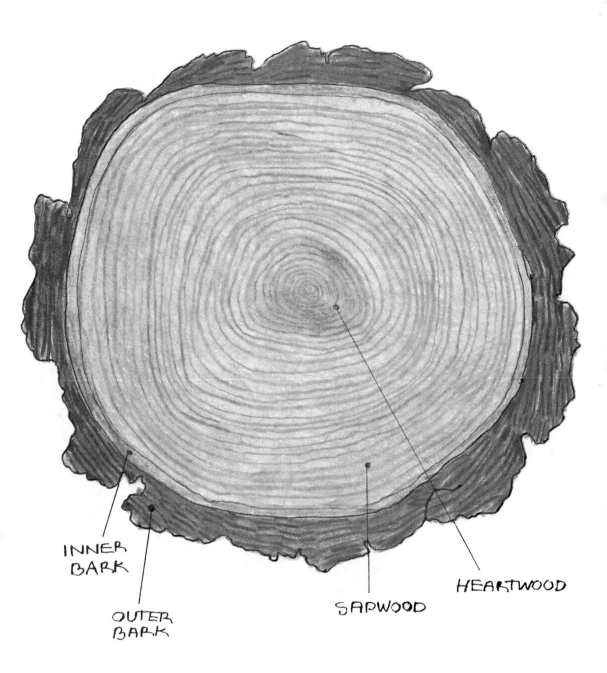

INNER
BARK

OUTER
BARK

SAPWOOD

HEARTWOOD

This tree was 35 years old.

The *roots* of a tree grow from under the trunk into the ground. They anchor the tree, keeping it in place.

At the tip of the roots are *root hairs*. The walls of the root hairs are so thin that water can pass through them. The water often has minerals in it that are valuable to the tree.

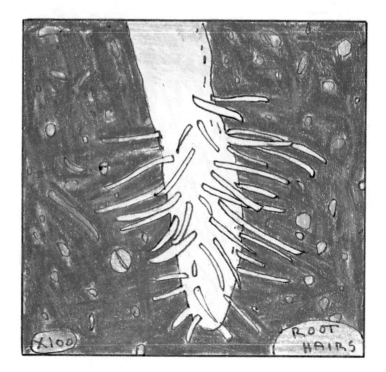

While the roots are working underground, the leaves of the tree are busy above the ground. A substance in the leaves called *chlorophyll* captures sunlight and mixes it with water and a part of the air called *carbon dioxide*. From these the chlorophyll makes plant foods called *sugars*. These tree sugars make fruit taste sweet.

x ½

GREY POPLAR

x2

ASPEN

The leaves of trees come in many different shapes. Pine and fir trees have thin leaves, like this silver fir.

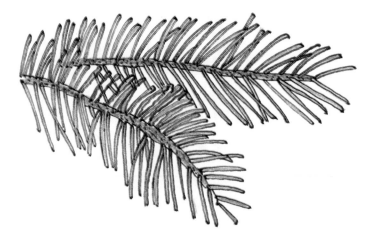

Other trees have wide leaves, like this sycamore.

Some leaves are divided into smaller leaves called *leaflets*. The black locust tree has many leaflets.

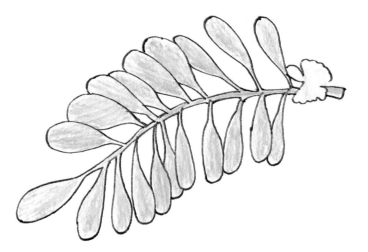

The edges of some leaves are rough, like this elm tree leaf. Others have smooth edges, like these live oak leaves.

All trees have seeds. They are kept in cones, flowers, or fruit. Most trees with cones are *evergreens*. Their leaves stay green all year long, even when it gets cold. This is the cone of the red fir tree. It's found in Oregon and in California.

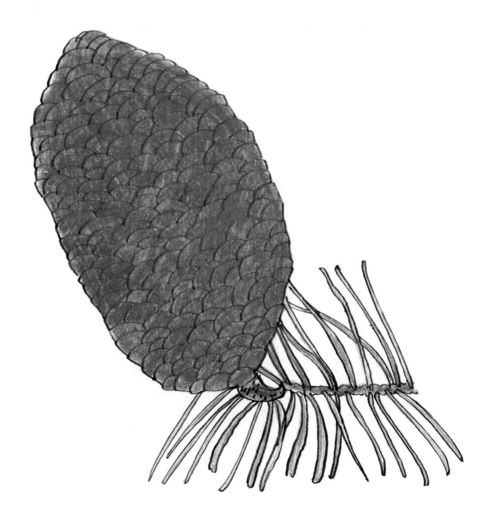

MAGNOLIA

Some trees have showy flowers to attract bees and butterflies and other insects. This is the flower of the magnolia tree. The insects collect pollen and nectar and pollinate the flowers. Later the flowers turn into fruit and seeds. Some seeds are blown away by the wind, and new trees grow far away from the older tree. Some seeds are carried away by animals.

Birds or animals often help spread seeds by eating the fruit of trees. This is the fruit of the cherry.

NORWAY MAPLE

Most trees with flowers have wider leaves than the thin leaves of evergreens. They are called *broadleaf* trees. When the weather gets cold, their leaves die. They may change color before they fall to the ground. In the spring new leaves grow from *buds*.

X5

ROYAL PALMS

PUERTO RICO

The place in the world where a tree grows naturally is called its *habitat*. Some trees, like palm trees, need a hot, sunny climate. Their long trunks help them grow above other trees and get more sun.

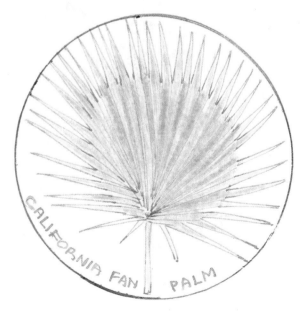

The baobab tree of Africa lives in a very dry habitat. Its thick trunk can store rain water for long periods of time.

The bald cypress is one of the few trees that can grow
in water. It is also found in moist soil. This tree loses its
leaves in November.

Sometimes a tree is planted by people in a place outside of its natural habitat. The gingko tree once grew only in China. Later it was planted in Japan, Europe, and America. Its beautiful leaves are shaped like a fan.

The date palm tree originally grew only in Asia and North Africa. Now it grows in Florida and in California as well. People enjoy eating the fruit of this tree, the date.

Trees that are similar are said to belong to the same tree *family*. The pine family includes more than 250 kinds of trees. All pines have very thin flat leaves called *needles*. And they all have cones to hold their seeds.

The sugar pine, found in Oregon and in California, is the tallest pine. It grows up to 200 feet, and its cones can be 24 inches long.

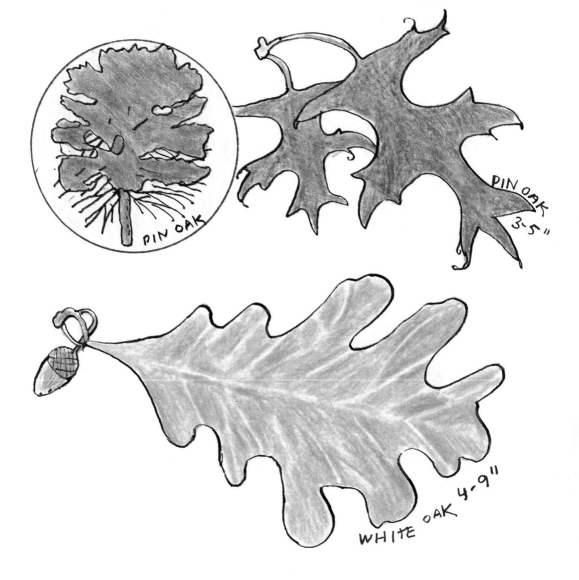

The pin oak, like other oak trees, has acorns. The acorns sit in cups that have scales. This tree always has a few branches near its bottom that grow downward and have no leaves. The twigs of these branches look like pins.

The trunk and branches of the white oak grow much larger than those of the pin oak. Another difference is that the white oak's leaves are rounder and larger.

The elm family is found throughout the world, but it is most common in North America. The leaves of elms have rough edges and are uneven at the bottom.

The American elm is shaped like a vase. It was once very common in the United States, but many trees died from Dutch elm disease.

Willows are usually found in cooler climates. They have very long leaves and small green flowers. The branches of willows bend easily. Sometimes they are used to make baskets.

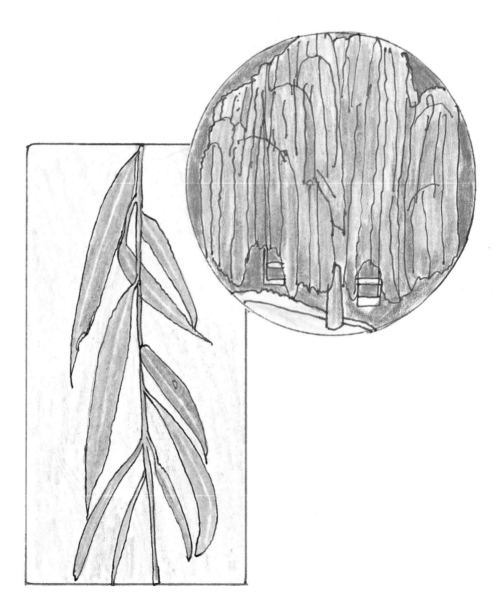

Trees are very useful to us. Their wood is needed to make homes, furniture, rubber, paper, boats, baseball bats, and thousands of other things. Apples, peaches, oranges, and other fruit all grow on trees. So do many kinds of nuts.

The future of trees is largely in the hands of all of us. Millions of trees are cut down each year for lumber and paper, and to clear land. Air pollution and water pollution are also killing many trees. Even rain can be so polluted that it harms trees.

Many animals and plants depend on trees to survive. Trees put oxygen into the air we breathe. They keep the soil rich with nutrients. Trees hold rain water in the ground and prevent floods.

Best of all, trees make our world a more beautiful place in which to live.

ORANGE

To Marie and Alegria

Copyright © 1986 by Douglas Florian
All rights reserved. No part of this book may be reproduced or transmitted in any form or by any
means, electronic or mechanical, including photocopying, recording, or by any information storage
and retrieval system, without permission in writing from the Publisher.
Aladdin Books
Macmillan Publishing Company
866 Third Avenue, New York, NY 10022
Collier Macmillan Canada, Inc.
First Aladdin Books edition 1990
Printed in the United States of America
A hardcover edition of Discovering Trees is available from Charles Scribner's Sons,
Macmillan Publishing Company.

10 9 8 7 6 5 4 3 2

Library of Congress Cataloging-in-Publication Data

Florian, Douglas.
Discovering trees/Douglas Florian. — 1st Aladdin Books ed.
p.   cm.
Reprint. Originally published: New York: Scribner, © 1986.
Summary: An introduction to trees, their growth, reproduction,
usefulness, and some specific kinds.
ISBN 0-689-71377-0
1. Trees — Juvenile literature. [1. Trees] I. Title.
[QK475.8.F56 1990]
582.16 — dc20   89-37817   CIP   AC